Fatherhood by George

GEORGE FOREMAN

WITH MAX DAVIS

Thomas Nelson™
Since 1798

NASHVILLE DALLAS MEXICO CITY RIO DE JANEIRO BEIJING

Fatherhood by George
© 2008 by George Foreman

All rights reserved. No portion of this book may be reproduced, stored in a retrieval system, or transmitted in any form or by any means—electronic, mechanical, photocopy, recording, scanning, or other—except for brief quotations in critical reviews or articles, without the prior written permission of the publisher.

Published in Nashville, TN, by Thomas Nelson. Thomas Nelson is a trademark of Thomas Nelson, Inc.

Thomas Nelson, Inc., titles may be purchased in bulk for educational, business, fundraising, or sales promotional use. For information, please email SpecialMarkets@ThomasNelson.com.

Unless otherwise noted, all scripture references are from *The King James Version*. © 1979, 1980, 1982, 1992, Thomas Nelson, Inc., Publisher. Used by permission. *The New International Version* (NIV) © 1984 by the International Bible Society. Used by permission of Zondervan Bible Publishers. *The Message* (MSG) © 1993. Used by permission of NavPress Publishing Group. *The Holy Bible, New Living Translation* (NLT) © 1996. Used by permission of Tyndale House Publishers, Inc., Wheaton, Ill. All rights reserved. *The King James Version of the Bible* (KJV).

Published in association with the literary agency of Mark Sweeney & Associates, Bonita Springs, Florida 34135.

Designed by the DeisgnWorks Group, www.thedesignworksgroup.com

ISBN-13: 978-14041-0421-1

Printed in the United States of America

May you follow the Father
to become the father
you've always wanted to be.

TABLE OF CONTENTS

Nothing I've ever
done has given me more joys
and rewards than being a
father to my children.

BILL COSBY

BEING THERE

I am by no means a perfect father. I've made plenty of mistakes and had to apologize to my kids many times, just like every father who has ever lived. But I've always done my very, very best. When I became a father, I was absolutely determined that my kids would have their dad's guiding presence in their lives. I didn't want them growing up without their father's influence, the way I did.

I am blessed to have such a wonderful mother, but kids—and I was one of them—will wear out any parent who is trying to be both mother and father.

In this little book—that I hope packs a big punch—I want to share some of the things I've learned about being a dad. You don't have to agree with all of them to get something out of this book. In fact, a few people say I can get a little controversial for being such a nice guy!

Fatherhood is so rewarding and challenging—and so very important—and I want to share with you what I've learned about how to win kids' hearts, build them up and nurture their strengths and abilities, and give them boundaries and a clear a path to follow.

We can't shirk these responsibilities. Our kids are thirsty for our love and approval. They need the security of a dad's strength and guidance. They need role models. And they desperately need our prayers and attention. If we don't step in and fulfill our role as fathers, who can we really count on, who else can we really trust to be there for them if their lives run off course? I'm not saying we can do it all or that others won't step in to lend a hand, but I for one plan to be there for my kids.

I hope this book encourages you to keep on working to make your kids' lives better. Everything you do as a father matters. No matter what has happened in the past, choose today to become the best father you can be.

Step one is just being there for them.

RUN FOR YOUR LIFE

My children, listen when your father corrects you.
Pay attention and learn good judgment,
for I am giving you good guidance.

PROVERBS 4:1–2 NLT

1

Drifting out in space, isolated, far away from the gravitational pull of the earth—just hanging around without direction, nothing to keep me grounded—no course to run on, no path to follow. That's what it felt like for me growing up fatherless. What I lacked and desperately needed was the strong arm of guidance, that stabilizing, grounding force that only a loving father can give.

My mama tried her best to fulfill the roles of both mother and father. She was wonderful and tender, giving me all of her gentle love and care. Because I was so big, Mama always saw to it that I had a little extra food. She'd even let me eat off her plate. Like most good mothers, she sacrificed much for me and would do just about anything for her boy. Yet there was one thing Mama couldn't do no matter how hard she tried: she couldn't be a father. Oh, how she longed to be that strong arm of guidance that I needed, but as I grew older and more adamant, she would often fall short. Eventually, my rebellious and stubborn nature, coupled with my intimidating size, simply wore her down. In the end, all she could do was turn me over to the Lord. I can remember that day so vividly. Mama, frustrated and tired, looked up at her teenage giant and said, "Son, I just can't do it anymore. You're too much to handle. I'm turning you over to the Lord."

Now, that may not sound very threatening to some, but make no mistake about it, turning me over to the Lord was not a passive move on her part. It was something my mama took very seriously. She knew she couldn't manhandle me or protect me from the pressures and temptations of the world anymore. So, through the tears and pain that only a loving mother can know, she committed herself to prayer, leaving me to the Lord for Him to do whatever He needed in order to get my attention. And I'm here to tell you that the Lord answered her prayers.

In the scripture at the beginning of this chapter, Solomon, the author, plainly shows it is the father's job to guide his children and that children are smart when they pay attention to fatherly advice. And although Solomon's writing was directed to the children of God universally, as he continued to develop his thoughts in this passage he wrote about the impact his own father, David, had in his life: *"My children, listen when your father corrects you. Pay attention and learn good judgment, for I am giving you good guidance. Don't turn away from my instructions. For I too, was once my father's son, tenderly loved as my mother's only child.*

My father taught me, 'Take my words to heart. Follow my commands, and you will live'" (Proverbs 4:1–4 NLT). What did David mean when he told his son Solomon, *"Take my words to heart. Follow my commands and you will live"?* In essence, he meant that it was his responsibility as a father to lead and direct his son in the ways of life, to a place where he could reach

> *The call of fatherhood is to be a strong arm of guidance— a consistent blend of love, strength, respect, friendship, teaching, and discipline.*

his full potential as a person, and by heeding his father's advice, Solomon could avoid the pitfalls that lead to destruction.

The call of fatherhood is to be a strong arm of guidance—a consistent blend of love, strength, respect, friendship, teaching, and discipline. But when the father-presence is absent and the mother is unable to fulfill the role, God often has to use other methods as the strong arm of direction. Many times those other methods are brutal. For me, those methods began with a run-in with the law.

After Mama had turned me over to the Lord, it didn't take very long for the Lord to start working. On one particular night the police were looking for me because I'd been involved in an illegal activity. To say I was scared would have been an understatement. I was terrified—more than I had been in my entire life. So, as a reaction to my fear, I instinctively started to run. The whole time I was running, a voice kept thundering in my mind and I knew it was the voice of God. He told me, "Okay, George, you want to run from rules? You want to run from authority and from what your mother says? Well, George, let's run now. Let's run for your life."

God told me, "You want to run from authority and from what your mother says? Well, George, let's run now. Let's run for your life."

Up to that point, I had seen myself as invincible, that nothing could really happen to me. Yet there I was, running for my life, from the police, trying to find a place to hide. They were chasing me like I was a common criminal, and I knew if I got caught that I was going straight to jail. They even had dogs with them to sniff me out. While trying to hide, a scene from a movie replayed in my mind. Some escaped prisoners were running from tracking dogs, and they jumped into a creek to break their scent. With this scene playing in my mind, I crawled into a busted sewer pipe and laid there, hoping the dogs wouldn't smell me. Hiding there in that foul, stinky, nasty pipe, hearing the cops' voices getting closer and closer, thinking about those dogs coming at me, tearing me apart and then going to jail, for the first time it dawned on me that I was no different from those men in the movie. I had done wrong and I was a criminal. All the things Mama had told me started coming to my mind, especially, "George, I'm turning you over to the Lord." It was then that I said to myself, *"If I get out of this sewer pipe, I will never break the law again. I'm going to make something of my life!"* Looking back, that was the beginning of my transformation, but it took many years and the Lord using many more of life's hard methods for me to learn what I needed to learn. Years later, when I became a father myself, I determined I was going to be that strong arm of guidance and stabilizing, grounding force that my children would need in their lives.

THE LASTING IMPACT OF FATHERLESSNESS

The impact of fatherlessness in our world today is far reaching—from high-paid athletes doing foolish things, to inmates in maximum security prisons, to children making poor life choices. Consider for a moment the raw statistics. Roughly

85 percent of youth in prison today come from fatherless homes. Ninety percent of homeless kids or runaways are fatherless. Sixty-three percent of youth suicides were fatherless, as are 71 percent of high school dropouts.[1]

Often when I go into prisons to minister or I'm counseling a professional athlete, it becomes obvious to me that many of them are craving a father figure. They may be big and physical on the outside, but inside there's a little boy asleep who doesn't know what to do. They're reaping the effects of poor choices, and I believe a significant reason they've made these poor choices is because of the absence of a father figure in their lives. Every child growing up desperately needs a David or Solomon who will say to them and model before them, "Take my words to heart. Follow my commands, and you will live." And that is what this book is all about. Whether you're a brand new father, a father of a teenager, or even a seasoned veteran of an adult child, it's about you seizing the moment and becoming the father-presence God intended you to be. Think about it. If fatherlessness has the power to affect our world in such a negative way, then imagine the influence a loving father has to shape his children and thus the world in a positive way. Ken Canfield couldn't have said it better when he wrote in his book *The Heart of a Father*, "A father has enormous power. About this, he has no choice. For good or for bad, by his presence or absence, action or inaction, whether abusive or nurturing, the fact remains: A father is one of the most powerful beings on the face of the earth."[2]

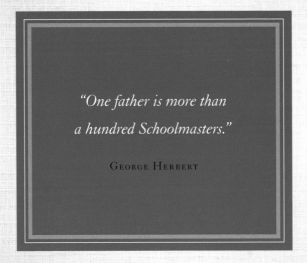

"One father is more than a hundred Schoolmasters."

GEORGE HERBERT

MAKE HOME A REFUGE

I established the George Foreman Youth and Community Center in 1984 in part to create a safe haven for fatherless and street kids to hang out. Financing the project was one of my reasons for jumping back into the ring.

As good fathers we need to make home a haven—a refuge where our kids like to hang out. A place they'll miss when they're gone, not someplace they'll remember with grief. We must work to make our homes places where our kids can retreat when they need comfort and acceptance, regardless of their age. They should feel safe at home no matter what's going on in the outside world. They need to be able to relax and let down their guard.

As fathers we want our homes to be centers of compassion and hope for our children, not sources of pain and frustration. The physical structure of a home doesn't have to be fancy or crammed with all the latest technology. It simply needs to be warm, restful, and filled with love. You might be thinking, "Isn't that the mother's job?" It's true, mothers are the primary nurturers and nest builders, but as the leader of your family you set the tone for what happens in your home. Making a house a home for our children is not a mother's job; it's a responsible parent's job.

Recently a survey asked college students why they liked or disliked going home. Their answers are simple, but should challenge us fathers.

I LIKE GOING BACK HOME BECAUSE:

- I miss the good food.
- I like to watch sports with my dad.
- I can relax and forget about the stress of school.

- I know my parents love me unconditionally.
- I like sleeping in my bed.
- My parents pamper me when I go home. It's like a vacation.
- I like sitting around the dinner table with my family and talking about what's going on in our lives.
- I can talk to my parents about issues in my life. They're really good about listening and giving me wise advice. They don't lecture or pressure me.
- I like the smell of our house when I walk in the door.

I DON'T LIKE TO GO HOME BECAUSE:
- My parents fight.
- My parents nag me a lot.
- My parents pry into love life. They're so worried I won't get married.
- My parents complain about everything.
- My parents are always down because of their own problems.
- No one's ever there. My parents are busy with their own lives. But that's the way it's always been.
- My faith has become very important to me. My parents are not supportive of my spiritual choices.
- I can't do anything right. I'm tired of hearing that.[3]

Which of these answers sound like something your child would say? What are you going to do about it?

DO YOU REALLY WANT IT?

*Pray that I'll know what to say
and have the courage to say it
at the right time.*

EPHESIANS 6:19 MSG

2

Fatherhood is not an easy assignment. It's tough! As the father of five boys and five girls, and the grandfather of a growing number of grandchildren, I can readily testify to that fact. Being a loving, fully present father takes courage, lots of courage. You have to stand strong and secure in the face of opposition. You must defend, protect, sacrifice, make unpopular decisions, take the pressure, carry the load, while at the same time being loving, wise, and understanding. Successful fatherhood seems an impossible task. Well, the truth is, it is impossible . . . impossible without the help of the good Lord, that is. Only the Lord can give us the strength and wisdom we'll need to do this right. I'm constantly finding myself going before the Lord, seeking His direction for my fatherhood. "Lord, give me the courage and wisdom to say and do the right thing. Help me make the correct decision in this situation. Then, Lord, please give me the strength and courage to carry it out." Knowing what to do and doing it are two different things. We fathers are always being watched, and our children know when we're being inconsistent or insincere. Being a consistent leader and mentor takes stamina, determination, and, like I said earlier, courage.

Fatherhood is filled with wonderful blessings too numerous to count. But those blessings are also mixed with frustration and pain.

Please don't get me wrong. Fatherhood is an awesome thing! It's filled with many priceless moments of joy and satisfaction. And the Bible does say, "Children are a gift from the Lord; they are a reward from Him" (Psalm 127:3 NLT). It's true, they are a blessing, but many times the blessing comes disguised in packages that we won't fully understand until later in this life or even in the next life.

Yes, fatherhood is filled with wonderful blessings too numerous to count. But those blessings are also mixed with frustration and pain. That's why at times it would be easier to just give up and check out. Unfortunately, many fathers today have done just that, checked out. Some have checked out physically, choosing to not be involved in their children's lives or activities. They rarely, if ever, come around.

Oh, they'll send child support payments, but only because the law requires it. Some fathers may be present bodily, but they've checked out emotionally. For a variety of reasons they're out of touch with their children and the problems they're facing. They may be seen, but they're not effective as the strong arm of guidance that they're called to be. In his book *Anchor Man*, Steve Farrar wrote "Physical distance from your children is toxic; emotional distance from your children is even more toxic."[4] Someone else once said that any male can spawn a child, but it takes a real man to be a father.

I was put to the father test when one of my daughters was sixteen and I had to make the hard decision to discipline her by taking away her car for an extended period. The next day she had to ride the bus to school rather than drive. It was a humbling experience for her. That morning, pulling out of the driveway, I had to drive by the bus stop where she was waiting with some other kids. When I drove by and my precious daughter saw me, she very coldly and deliberately turned her back to me. Now, you have to understand, this was one of my babies. We were close and had that special father-daughter bond. Yet for over a month, she held a grudge and barely even talked to me. When she did, she'd use very short, cutting, begrudging responses. Let me tell you something, friend. That hurt! I can't begin to tell you how much. But you know what? God gave me the strength to stand my ground because I knew the decision to suspend her driving privileges was in her best interest. And even though she was mad at me, deep in her heart she knew I was still her daddy and I was going to be there for her. That's part of successful fathering. A secure father lets his children get mad, allows them space to work through their issues while he stands strong and makes himself available. He patiently endures the hurt, knowing that in time the child will come around. Of course, sometimes the situations are much more serious than this and involve tougher consequences and deeper pain, but the principle is the same: you do what's best for your child even when it hurts.

Our goal is to influence our children, not to control them.

Back in the 1970s during a boxing match, I was faced with a personal challenge. After about three rounds I was getting pounded really hard and was on the verge of being knocked out. Staggering back to my corner, I plopped down on the stool, and my manager, Gil Clancy, began slapping me in the face to wake me up. "George!" he shouted. "Do you want it? George, do you really want it!" Right there in the ring, I had to decide whether or not to fight—either surrender to the pain or get back in the ring and give it my best shot. It was up to me. Did I really want it? Did I really want to go the distance?

Today, when my kids resist me and respond by doing and saying hurtful things, when I'm getting pounded pretty good in a "boxing match" with them, when I see them getting hurt by life, when fatherhood just breaks me down to crying and I'm tempted to just check out, I ask myself, "George, do you really want it? Do you really want to be a good father?"

You, my friend, have to ask yourself that same question. "Do you really want it? Do you really want to be a good father?" If so, be prepared to go the distance. As soon as you answer, "Yes, I want it," then the pain eases and courage miraculously takes its place.

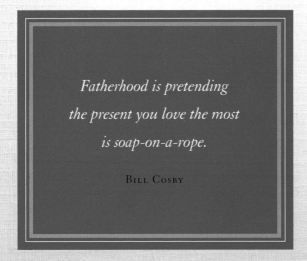

Fatherhood is pretending the present you love the most is soap-on-a-rope.

BILL COSBY

KEEP YOURSELF
UNDER CONTROL

One of the first cardinal rules of boxing is keeping your body under control. A proper stance is the key to executing all the boxing moves correctly. Your body must be relaxed and yet under control. If you're not under control, your opponent gains an advantage.

The same is true in raising our children. If you're not under control, you lose your ability to lead and influence. The apostle Paul understood this life principle when he said, *"I discipline my body and bring it into submission, lest, when I have preached to others, I myself should become disqualified"* (1 Corinthians 9:27). In essence, Paul was saying he's careful to keep his body and emotions under control so he can continue being an effective minister. A lack of control would disqualify him for the role.

In fatherhood, learning to be under control means being deliberate about the decisions we make and the things we say. I am not saying we never make mistakes; this isn't about trying to be flawless—this is recognizing that no one, not even our kids, can make us react in certain ways. Our reactions are up to us. Period. When we let our children press our buttons or push us over the edge, it's our fault, not theirs. Our emotional responses are always up to us. We can always choose how to react.

In boxing, one surefire way to lose control is allowing anger to take over. The same is true with our kids. Responding in anger is a surefire way to lose your influence. Here are a few pointers to help you control your anger when you're tempted to explode.

- *Calm yourself.* Count to ten very slowly and take a few deep breaths before responding. Focus on the counting and breathing, not on what your kid is doing. It sounds too simple, I know, but you'd be amazed at how much you can calm down in those few seconds.

- *Get away from the situation.* Take a walk or run. Go to the health club or the grocery store. Do something that will allow you to cool down. Often our whole perspective changes after we've cooled off.

- *Talk to God.* Ask Him how you should respond. He's ready and willing to impart wisdom to you. James 1:5 tells us, *"If any of you lacks wisdom, he should ask God, who gives generously to all without finding fault, and it will be given him"* (NIV).

NO LINES IN THE SAND

*But while he was still a long way off,
his father saw him and was filled with
compassion for him; he ran to his son, threw
his arms around him and kissed him.*

LUKE 15:20 NIV

3

Once you have answered "Yes, I really want it" then you have to realize that fatherhood is a lifetime assignment. It never ends. Your role will change depending on your children's ages, but you will always be their father and will have an influence, sometimes more so after your children are grown. Choosing to go the distance is one of the greatest things you will ever do for your children.

One of my favorite stories in the Bible is the parable of the Prodigal Son (Luke 15:11–32). Typically people focus on the failures and indiscretions of the son as he hits rock bottom and finally comes to his senses. But in reality, it's as much about the father's outrageous patience, love, and grace. No doubt, the son wounded his father deeply when he rejected the family, took his inheritance, and left to go make some pretty stupid life choices. The father was grieved by his son's actions, yet he responded with compassion, forgiveness, and grace when his son deserved it the least. I like the way Brennan Manning described the scene in his book *The Ragamuffin Gospel*:

> "For me, the most touching verse in the entire Bible is the father's response: 'While he was still a long way off, his father saw him and was moved with pity. He ran to the boy, clasped him in his arms and kissed him tenderly' (Luke 15:20). I am moved that the father didn't cross-examine the boy, bully him, lecture him on ingratitude, or insist on any high motivation. He was so overjoyed at the sight of his son that he ignored all the canons of prudence and parental discretion and simply welcomed him home. The father took him back just as he was."[5]

> *Fatherhood is a lifetime assignment. It never ends.*

One of the things I've learned in my many years of fatherhood is if you are going to raise children and maintain a loving relationship with them, you can't draw lines that result in alienation. You know what I mean? You give them an ultimatum such as, "If you cross this line that's it. I'm finished." No, no, no. Drawing lines is more about exercising power and control than about providing loving, caring guidance. Discipline, unlike drawing lines, means to instruct and train your kids so they will learn the self control to later guide themselves. A loving father either draws another line when they cross the first one, or he doesn't draw lines at all. In order to continue to have input in your child's life you have to keep the lines of communication open and maintain an attitude of grace.

Picture it in your mind. This smart-alecky kid takes his father's money and just splits. "Adios, Dad, I'm done with you!" In that time and culture it was the equivalent of saying, "You're dead to me, Dad." But the father doesn't say, "That's it, Son. You've really blown it now. You've crossed the line. I'm finished with you." No, he lets his breaking heart fill with both pain and forgiveness, watches his son leave, and then hopes and prays that one day his son comes to his senses and returns.

What I really like in the story is how, after seeing his son in the distance, the father runs to him. I can just picture this dad in his robe and sandals running down the dirt road. It was quite an undignified sight. The father left himself wide open to criticism and vulnerable to rejection. He didn't stop to analyze the situation, he simply reacted. But he didn't care. He loved his son that much. At the heart of every great father is love—love running through the dirt with its robe pulled up. And you know, for the son to come back, he had to have known deep down inside that he had a loving father waiting for him.

Whenever I'm tempted to give up on one of my children, I try to remember how patient God the Father has been with me— all those years of running, causing pain for Mama and a whole lot of other people. When I consider my own life, I'm forever amazed at how much patience and grace God, the Father, Abba, Daddy, has given me. It's important to remember this when fathering our own kids. If God had given up on me I wouldn't be here right now. He had plenty of chances to give up on me, to draw lines in the sand and say, "Okay, George, you've crossed the line. I'm done with you." But He never did and never does. No matter how much we've blown it, God is always standing there with arms open wide offering His grace if we will accept it. When I'm broken and bruised by this life, God the Father always says, "Welcome back, George." Jesus told His disciples to forgive someone seventy times seven (Matthew 18:22). That's keeping the relationship open, not drawing lines, and that's how we should father our children.

It took years to finally get my life turned around. God gave me many second chances. I'd been through four divorces, bankruptcy, devastating losses in the boxing ring. You name it, I'd done it. But God didn't give up on me, and now I've been happily married to Joan for over twenty years, bounced back financially, and, most importantly, begun living out God's calling on my life.

Why have I told you all this, and how does it relate to fatherhood? Well, we can learn how to treat our kids by the way God treats His kids. And that is: Discipline them, yes. Teach them, yes. Give them boundaries, yes. Give them consequences, too. But never ever give up on them, even when they've mistreated you or made poor life choices and are reaping their consequences. We have to let our fatherhood be strong and secure, but smothered in grace.

I'm glad a man named Charles "Doc" Broadus didn't give up on me. When I first gave boxing a chance while I was in the Job Corps, Doc was head of security at one of the Job Corps Training Centers, and he also oversaw the facility's boxing program. I was this brawny street kid with a mean, bullying attitude, and I got into fights all the time. But Doc saw something in me that no one else could see.

At the heart of every great father is love—love running through the dirt with its robe pulled up.

Doc considered me son. He had a lot of other young men to look after, many of whom were much better athletes than I was, but for some reason, Doc believed in me. And he helped me believe in myself.

Growing up in a tough neighborhood, I knew how to hit people with my fists, but boxing was a whole new game. Although I had size and strength, I didn't know how to correctly throw punches and defend myself. Doc had to start working with me from scratch. Boxing required more than just being able to bludgeon an opponent into submission. When Doc put me in the ring with a skinny guy, I figured I would chew him up in a matter of seconds. I went after him with a vengeance, throwing punches in every direction, assuming I'd knock out the boy with one punch. Maybe I would have, if any of the punches had landed. But the boy knew something I didn't—he knew how to box, not just fight. He kept circling around me, bobbing and weaving, hitting me hard but never allowing himself to be hit. Becoming more and more frustrated, I lunged at the boy, throwing a punch with all my might . . . and hit nothing but air. My momentum carried me forward, and, totally off balance, I fell awkwardly to the mat. Again and again I went after him, with much the same results. The guys around the ring were laughing hysterically, some of them holding their sides from laughing so much. When it was all over, Doc didn't say anything. He just let the lesson sink in. I left the gym quickly and didn't go back. I wanted to quit. I'd been embarrassed enough and now had to fight even more ferociously in the dorm to silence the guys who had witnessed the skinny kid beat the daylights out of the Job Corps bully.[6]

But Doc encouraged me not to give up, and with his help I began training. As I gained experience, I fought in the Diamond Belt competition sponsored by the Job Corps and won a bunch of trophies.

I want to father my children with the same grace the prodigal son's father had and with the same faith Doc had in me.

Don't draw lines with your kids. Never give up on them. As a loving father, you will be exposed to criticism and rejection from your kids, but you must maintain an attitude of grace to have influence and not alienate them.

> *When I was a boy of fourteen,*
> *my father was so ignorant*
> *I could hardly stand to have*
> *the old man around.*
> *But when I got to be*
> *twenty-one, I was astonished*
> *at how much he had*
> *learned in seven years.*
>
> MARK TWAIN

16 JABS YOU
SHOULD NEVER USE
ON YOUR KIDS

1. You'll never amount to anything.

2. You got what you deserved.

3. What's wrong with you?

4. You can't do anything right.

5. All you ever do is cause trouble.

6. Just wait until you have kids.

7. When will you ever learn?

8. You're stupid.

9. You'll be the death of me yet.

10. You need to have your head examined.

11. You don't care about anything.

12. What makes you think you are so special?

13. I can't wait until you are outta here!

14. Why can't you be more like your sister/brother?

15. I don't know why I had kids.

16. How could you do this to me?

Let no corrupt word proceed
out of your mouth, but what is good
for necessary edification,
that it may impart grace to the hearers.

Ephesians 4:29

PLANT SEEDS
OF GREATNESS

Death and life are in the power of the tongue.

PROVERBS 18:21 KJV

4

My parents split up when I was just a young boy. Whenever my father was around he usually drank heavily and fought with my mother. Because he squandered most of his money away on alcohol, Mama was left with the responsibility of providing for us kids. But despite his faults, I still longed to be accepted by my father.

Early in my life, my father planted a seed of greatness in my mind about my future. As we played, he often raised my hands over my head as if I had just won a boxing match, and he'd shout, "George Foreman, heavyweight champion of the world! Stronger than Jack Johnson. Hits like Jack Dempsey!" Even though I didn't understand what "heavyweight champion of the world" meant, he planted an idea in my mind that eventually became a reality.

It's incredible that he declared those things about me, almost like a prophecy about my future. It's even more amazing that not only would I become heavyweight champion, but I also came back from retirement and won it a second time twenty years later. My father started proclaiming my destiny when I was only four years old, and he continued saying it whenever he was around until I was a teenager.

You have power to shape your children's destinies by speaking encouraging words about who they are and who they can aspire to be.

A father's words can have a powerful influence in the life of a child, even an absentee father like mine. Imagine the power a loving, fully present father's words can have. You have power to shape your children's destinies by speaking encouraging words about who they are and who they can aspire to be, not merely what they already can do.

Fathers who lived during the Old Testament days blessed their children concerning their futures. They believed the prophetic words spoken over them would one day come to pass. In those days, the people believed strongly in the power of the father's blessings. When a family's father was getting up in years or approaching death, the sons would gather around him. Then, after laying his hands on each of them, the father would declare prophetic words over their lives.

Just as those Old Testament patriarchs blessed their children, fathers today can speak words of blessing to their kids as well. A father does not have to wait until old age to declare blessings over his children. He can speak encouraging words over them their whole lives. Tell them, "You're going to do well in life. God has good plans for you. You are a champion!"[7]

That doesn't mean you shouldn't speak words of correction. With my own children it seems like I have to get after them about something every day. When kids do something wrong, parents have a responsibility to correct them. But always remember to apply an equal amount of time to encouraging them. Just as positive words can build a child up, negative words can inflict pain, tear down, and wound a child's spirit, hindering them from achieving their full potential and what God has called them to be. It's our duty to teach and discipline our children when they make wrong choices. But we shouldn't badger or provoke them. Scripture warns us, *"Fathers, do not exasperate your children"* (Ephesians 6:4 NIV).

Our words can penetrate to the depths of our children's souls.

Whether or not we like it, fathers have enormous power for good or bad, especially with our words. Our words can penetrate to the depths of our children's souls. Listen to Proverbs 10:11: *"The mouth of the righteous is a well of life."* The words of a righteous father will be like cool, refreshing water that waters the roots of their children. Proverbs 18:21 says, *"Death and life are in the power of the tongue."* The words we speak to our children have the power to create life or death in them. By frequently speaking words of discouragement, we tear down a child's self-confidence. Think of all the adults today who are suffering because of the destructive things their parents spoke over them as children.

The Bible compares our tongue and the words we speak to the rudder of a large ship. It says, *"Take ships as an example. Although they are so large and are driven by strong winds, they are steered by a very small rudder wherever the pilot wants to go. Likewise the tongue is a small part of the body, but it makes great boasts"* (James 3:4–5 NIV). Although the rudder of a ship is small, by controlling it, the ship's captain guides the direction of the entire ship. This holds true for our lives personally and for our parenting. A father's words can help guide their children. Start guiding your children with your words and plant seeds of greatness in their lives.

My prescription for success
is based on something
my father always
used to tell me:
"You should never try
to be better than someone else,
but you should never cease
to be the best
that you can be."

JOHN WOODEN

BE CONSISTENT

In boxing training, as with other sports, one of the most important keys to success is being consistent in your workout routine. By being consistent, an average athlete can eventually become stronger, faster, and more skillful. There's great power in consistency. William Covington Jr. said, "There's a mysterious power in consistency. No one, no matter how gifted or talented, will achieve their potential in life without it." I would like to add to that thought by saying, not just any type of consistency will do. We must consistently practice the *correct* techniques. If we don't, we can work incredibly hard, with unyielding consistency, and still fail miserably. As it is in sports, successful fatherhood is rooted in consistently practicing good techniques with our children. Even the small things we do, again and again, add up over the years.

One of the principal reasons for consistency is to help our children to develop trust. Having a father they can unswervingly depend on to encourage, instruct, protect, and love them, is critical to their healthy development. Where there is no consistency, there cannot be trust. When a father is consistent in these areas it sends a message of reliability which promotes a sense of security and confidence in children. They know what to expect. It tells them that their father is for them regardless of the particular situation. The consistent father practices what he preaches. He follows through with his promises. by being consistent you give your children a safe base they can depend on and a place they can return to when the rest of their life gets chaotic. And remember this: being a consistent father not only creates stability for your children's lives, it creates stability and peace in yours as well.

And let us not grow weary
while doing good,
for in due season we shall reap
if we do not lose heart.

GALATIANS 6:9

A FATHER'S IMAGE

For in Christ Jesus I [Paul] became your
father through the gospel.
Therefore I urge you to imitate me.

1 CORINTHIANS 4:15–16 NIV

5

Because I've been a pastor for many years now, my children grew up in church with me. Most of the people who come to our fellowship are seeking answers, so they *want* to hear what I have to say. This is not necessarily true with my kids. They go to my church out of duty, because they're mine, because it's a rule. Going to church is not up for discussion. If you live under my roof, you go to church with me, period. What this means, in a very practical sense, is that sometimes their ears and eyes are not open to what I'm preaching. They're not really listening, nor are they paying much attention. Sometimes they pout and whine because they'd rather be someplace else. They're just going through the motions of church. So, why do I make them go? Am I being mean or unreasonable? I don't think so.

I make them go for several reasons. I'm hoping to establish a lifetime pattern in their lives and most importantly, I know that good seeds are being planted in them—that they are around other positive influences and are in an atmosphere of truth. My prayer is that when they are thirsty enough all those seeds will be watered by God's Spirit, resulting in spiritual growth.

As fathers, we must allow our kids the space and time to develop their own relationships with God.

Jesus said, *"If anyone is thirsty, let him come to me and drink"* (John 7:37 NIV). I've noticed that when people are thirsty for truth, they seek and find answers. Most of the people who come to my church are thirsty. That's why they come. But with my children, it's not my job to either make them thirsty or make them drink when they're not thirsty. I couldn't make them thirsty if I wanted to.

Many parents go wrong by trying to force their kids to be spiritual when they're not ready, and that leads to hypocrisy or a borrowed faith at best. You cannot force your child into a relationship with God. It would not be authentic. As fathers, we must allow our kids the space and time to develop their own relationships with God.

Our job as fathers is to plant good seeds and be an example. In God's own timing, our children *will* get thirsty, and, if we as good fathers have planted good seeds, then those seeds will soak in the water, take root, and bear spiritual fruit in our kids. The way we plant good seeds is twofold: by speaking truth and by modeling truth, living an authentic faith before them. Kids have an innate sense of knowing when something or someone is a fake, so our authenticity is vital.

The spoken word has power, but it has little *positive* power if our motto is, *"Do as I say, not as I do."* In this chapter I want to discuss the power of a father's lifestyle model. When I was very young, my father's words had a major impact on me. However, his lifestyle model had very little positive impact on me, especially later in my adolescence. This left me drifting with no specific direction. Before my parents split, I remember walking down the street one day with some friends and seeing my father staggering around drunk. He wobbled, then bobbed back and forth, and then passed out and fell into a ditch. I was ashamed for my friends to see my father in that condition. After we arrived where we were going, I slipped away from them and quickly ran back and pulled my father out of the

> *A father's presence is absolutely essential for positive role modeling. You have to be around for your children to see you!*

ditch.[8] This and many other similar incidences seared negative images in my mind. And like I said earlier, because of my father being absent during the most important season of my life, I felt as if I were floating around in outer space without anything to ground me. A father's presence is absolutely essential for positive role modeling. You have to be around for your children to see you! My children may not be listening when I preach, but you can bet your bottom dollar they're watching the way I live.

> *The best thing a father can do for his children is love their mother. This speaks volumes to our kids.*

For example, fathers can show their children how men are supposed to treat women by the way they treat their wives. I've always heard the best thing a father can do for his children is love their mother. This speaks volumes to our kids. If we treat our wives with dignity and respect, then our daughters will come to expect that from the men who come into their lives. All men will be held up to their "Daddy" standard and that can be a good thing. On the down side, if we model critical and demeaning attitudes and emotional unavailability, our daughters will inevitably set low standards, but they will also crave male acceptance and validation which can set them up for unhealthy relationships.

Another thing for us to remember about modeling is that most children shape their images and attitudes about God based on their fathers. That's a pretty tall responsibility. If our personalities are callous, overly critical, unreasonable, or addictive, our children will grow up with a warped image of God. If we are secure, loving, patient, and compassionate, our children will have a healthier understanding of God's true nature.

Marjorie Holmes wrote about her experience with her father in *How Can I Find You, God?*:

"This dad, this earthly father . . . looking back I find more pointers toward God in him than I realized. He was not complex, he was never remote. He was never too busy to listen to us. And though he sometimes got mad and yelled and was stern and we thought him unfair, we found out he wasn't. He was quick to forgive and he never held a grudge.

He loved us, was concerned about us, and was proud of us. He never let any of us down, not once . . . What more can anyone ask of a father? And if this is the nature of a good earthly father, why shouldn't the father of us all be just as easy to know and to trust?"[9]

Marjorie's experience with her father was good, but for

> *If we are secure, loving, patient, and compassionate, our children will have a healthier understanding of God's true nature.*

many children it is not so good. When many people think of their fathers, feelings of abuse, pain, abandonment, shame, and neglect flood their emotions. Maybe a person's father died or, like mine, was absent, leaving the children with a void. If this is the case, it is hard to picture God as good and loving. Mother Teresa wrote in *The Joy in Loving:*

"Vast regions of the world are covered by spiritual deserts. There you will find young people marked by human abandonment, the result of broken relationships, which affect them to their very depths. Even when they are thirsting for a spiritual life, many of the young are afflicted by doubt. They are unable to place their confidence in God, to believe, since they have not found confidence in those to whom life had entrusted them. Separations have wounded the innocence of their childhood or adolescence. The consequences are skepticism and discouragement. What's the use of living? Does life still have any meaning?"[10]

As the scripture at the beginning of this chapter indicates, the apostle Paul encouraged his followers in Christ to imitate him. We, as fathers, need to plant good seeds into our children's lives by modeling godly lifestyles before them, lives that we would feel honored for them to imitate.

Don't worry that
children never listen to you:
worry that they are
always watching you.

ROBERT FULGHUM

BE A COACH

Where would any good boxer or athlete be without his trainer or coach? I can't imagine where I'd be today without Charles "Doc" Broadus in my life. Doc was my original trainer and mentor. Oh, where would I be in life without the wisdom and love of that man!

Ara Parasheghian once said, "A good coach will make his players see what can be, rather than what they are." That's what Doc did for me, as well as instilling in me the knowledge that I needed in order to succeed in boxing. Knowledge like delivering effective body punches, dealing with getting hit, blocking, doing the Pendulum step, learning to read the signs of your opponent, creating openings, and executing jab taps. But most of all Doc taught me to believe in myself.

Good fathers are good coaches to their kids. They help their children see what they can be rather than what they are. Then dads instill in their kids the necessary knowledge to get them where they need to go. Teaching our children and coaching them through life is not an option. When God was giving His Law to the children of Israel, He told them, *"Teach them to your children, talking about them when you sit at home and when you walk along the road, when you lie down and when you get up"* (Deuteronomy 11:19 NIV). Simply put, it's God's will for fathers to teach their children about God and about life. And regardless of how sassy our children get, or how much they tell us that they already know, I believe that deep inside they really want to hear what we have to offer. I know I did. When I was fatherless, I would have given anything to have someone to teach me. I understand that some kids are more coachable than others, but the good coach, like the good father, stays at it. The following are some quick tips for being a good teacher/coach:

- *Be alert and watch for those teachable moments.* Sometimes kids don't want to be taught. Asking them to listen or sit down and talk can cause them to put up walls. But, if you are actively involved in their lives, little opportunities will open up. Watch out for those priceless moments. Over the years, they add up. Each day is a new opportunity to teach your child. Don't let time rob you of the moment.
- *Involve your children in the everyday activities of your life.* Making decisions, cooking healthy meals, managing money, maintaining your home and cars, reading the Bible and other good books, attending church, praying together, running errands, taking walks or exercising— these are natural ways to be with and communicate with your child without it being formal.
- *Be available.* Let your children know you are available to answer questions, help them, and participate in their lives.
- *Have fun.* Show your children that you enjoy being their father.
- *Tell your story.* This helps your children identify with you. Storytelling is often much more effective than teaching a lesson. Your life experiences can be useful tools in guiding your children. Plus, if they know that you have opened up to them, then they will feel more comfortable coming to you with their questions.
- *Use, don't hide, your mistakes.* You must be honest with your children. Admit your mistakes and teach them the value of taking personal responsibility and apologizing. This teaches them that it's not fatal to make mistakes and ask for forgiveness. When they see you taking responsibility, they are more likely to do it for themselves.

NEVER WISH TO BE IN ANYONE ELSE'S SHOES

6

Train up a child in the way he should go,
And when he is old he will not depart from it.

PROVERBS 22:6

I tell my kids to never wish to be in anyone's shoes but their own. Happiness and contentment have nothing to do with fame or fortune. True happiness and contentment come when we discover our God-given gifts and then begin developing them and walking in them. Greatness is about finding your purpose and celebrating it.

I've heard parents with the best of intentions tell their kids something like, "Little Johnny, you can do anything you want in life if you really set your mind to it." That statement sounds great and encouraging, but it can promote false hopes and can set up children for ultimate disappointment. The truth is, our kids can't do anything they want, no matter how much they set their minds to it. Little Johnny may want to be the next Michael Jordan, but if he doesn't have the raw tools and natural ability then he's not going to make it regardless of how many hours he spends in the gym. A better way to encourage and empower our kids is by saying something like, "Little Suzie, if you put your mind to discovering and developing your own unique God-given gifts, you will find happiness and contentment in life."

True happiness and contentment come when we discover our God-given gifts and then begin developing them and walking in them.

The famous child-rearing proverb is often misunderstood. It says, *"Train up a child in the way he should go, and when he is old he will not depart from it."* Generally we have taken this verse to mean that if we raise our children in a godly environment and teach them the Bible, then, even if at some point in their lives they rebel, eventually they will turn back to God. But that's not what the verse means. What it does mean is that our children are designed by God with certain strengths and gifts—a certain way or direction they are to go. They also have other areas of weakness—ways or directions they're not to go. It is our job as Christian parents to help our children discover, appreciate, and develop (train) their gifts, pointing them in the right direction or way.

To help our children discover their gifts and strengths, it's imperative that we spend time with them. If we don't spend time with them, we can't know them. We must pay attention to their interests and what they enjoy. Also, we must be willing to expose them to different opportunities by letting them try a variety of activities. Remember, it is as important to find out what our children's gifts are *not*, as what their gifts *are*. We have to let them know it's okay to fail—that failure is not fatal—as long as they use failure as a steppingstone to success. As much as we would like it to be true, our kids can't be good at everything. This process of discovering our kids' gifts can be exciting for all involved, and at some point along the journey things will begin to come into focus. But get ready to be surprised. God can be very creative when it comes to our children.

It is as important to find out what our children's gifts are not, *as what their gifts* are. *We have to let them know it's okay to fail—that failure is not fatal—as long as they use failure as a steppingstone to success.*

I never will forget when my daughter Freeda announced that she planned to become a boxer! Women's boxing was a growing sport, and Laila Ali and Jacqui Frazier-Lyde, daughters of Muhammad Ali and Joe Frazier, respectively, had already achieved some measure of success as boxers. Freeda figured she could do the same or better. I had my doubts and was against her boxing, but ultimately decided to let her try. I was hoping she would get it out of her system and move on.

God can be very creative when it comes to our children.

As a little girl, Freeda battled an even more formidable foe: food. Thanks to her mother and me, she learned early on that fries, hamburgers, pizza, ice cream, and other treats could make the best day even better. At that time in our lives we had little knowledge of what it meant to eat healthily. Although Freeda played sports in school, her growing weight problem caused her friends to shy away, and she began spending more and more time at home, snacking in front of a television.

We did everything we knew to help her—sending her to counseling, weight loss centers, nutritionists, and more. Nothing seemed to really evoke a successful lifestyle change. When she took up boxing, however, she started exercising and jogging several miles every day, and the weight began to fall off her body.

By the time she was scheduled for her first bout in Las Vegas, she was in tiptop shape and looked like a beautiful model.

Nevertheless, I still doubted her following my footsteps into the boxing ring. She was so pretty, and I couldn't stand the thought of my baby being punched. I tried my best to convince her to stay out of boxing, but she was insistent.

"Daddy, this is something I've always wanted to do," she said. I had playfully sparred with all my girls as they grew up, so boxing was not unfamiliar to them. But this was different: Freeda was stepping into the ring with another woman who wanted to knock her out!

To Freeda, boxing was about self-esteem and a sense of accomplishment. Overlooking my concerns, she stepped into the ring. But she wasn't there long. By 1:44 of the second round, Freeda had floored her opponent, LaQuanda Landers, and had won by a technical knockout. Believe it or not, it was Father's Day and after the fight, surrounded by the media, Freeda said, "Happy Father's Day, Daddy. This is for you. I love you."

By attentive listening, we let our children know they are worthy of our time—that we love and respect them and are interested in what they have to say.

Through boxing, Freeda discovered her true gifts and calling: working with youth. When she retired from boxing, she started working as the executive director at the George Foreman Youth and Community Center. Today, she visits schools and speaks to young people about developing good diet and exercise habits. She also emphasizes the importance of finding and hanging out with the right kinds of friends, and, of course, developing a friendship with God. Freeda developed "Freeda Foreman Family Fitness," a program to bring entire families together through health and fitness. She still holds the sport of boxing close to her heart and has hosted boxing matches at the center and has even promoted a number of amateur fights, including "Houston's Night of Stars." Freeda has become my right-hand person at the youth center and loves it.

God gives our children certain strengths and gifts for a purpose. As fathers, one of the most powerful things we can do for our children (even when we think they might fail!) is help them discover their gifts, develop them to their full potential, and help them build their lives around those gifts. If we do, our children will have full and contented lives.

*It is a wise father
that knows
his own child.*

WILLIAM SHAKESPEARE

PRACTICE ATTENTIVE
LISTENING

Attentive listening is one of the best ways fathers can influence their kids, and by attentive listening, I mean more than just being in the audible range of our kids' voices. Simply having ears is not enough to listen attentively or effectively. We also must listen with our hearts, our eyes, our whole beings. It means engaging our minds with our children. To fully understand what our children are telling us, we have to take the time and care to read them. What are their tones, inflections, feelings, and body language saying?

An important aspect of boxing is reading your opponent and finding a weakness in his technique that will help you gain an advantage. A good boxer watches films on their opponents to understand them better. They also train themselves to visualize and list all possible mistakes. A successful boxer knows his opponent well. Reading opponents is vital in boxing, and although our kids aren't our opponents, to be attentive listeners, we have to learn to read them. And to read them, we have to know them.

By attentive listening, we let our children know they are worthy of our time—that we love and respect them and are interested in what they have to say. However, too often we are more interested in making our own points than in really hearing what our children are saying. For fathers, the goal of attentive listening is to hear, understand, and accept what's on our children's hearts. If we want to truly grasp their thoughts and feelings, we must give up our right to lecture.

Here are some tips on attentive listening:

- Give your full attention.
- Don't minimize their feelings.
- Remain nonjudgmental.
- Be slow to respond.
- Realize that real listening takes effort.
- Realize that our children are not extensions of ourselves; they are individuals.
- Seek out meaningful information.
- Ask meaningful questions.
- Show understanding by restating.

THE BIGGEST
CHALLENGE

7

See then that you walk circumspectly,
not as fools but as wise, redeeming the time,
because the days are evil.

EPHESIANS 5:15–16 NKJV

As I've stated earlier in this little book, being a good father is a life*time* thing. You've probably heard it before, but I believe it's worth repeating: *Love* is spelled T-I-M-E. There's no greater way to love our children than by spending quality time with them. It's also true that finding time to do that is the biggest challenge to effective fatherhood. However, if we are going to be engaged fathers, then we *must* meet the challenge head on. To know our kids, to train them, to have a positive, lasting relationship with them, we just have to take some time—a little precious time. There is no other substitute. Do you want it? Do you really want it?

Like many fathers, I find that the more successful I am, the less time I have for my family. And with a career like mine, there are always plenty of opportunities to take on. What I'm learning, sometimes the hard way, is that I have to say "no" to some career things in order to be successful in family things. Not long ago, one of my sons was having an all-star season as running back for an undefeated team, but during that particular football season I was signed on to do a television show. Because of that career commitment, I did not get to see any of my son's games. He was so disappointed. All he wanted was to look up in the stands and see his father, to know that I was watching him. I can't begin to tell you how much I regret not getting to see my son break tackles and score touchdowns that year, but mostly I regret letting him down by not being where he could see me cheer him on. Now, I understand we can't *always* be there for our kids. It's not realistic. There are legitimate times when we just can't. However, in that particular instance I could make a choice. What did I need that show for? Was it really that important? My finances were secure. So, despite strong television ratings, I canceled my contract in order to spend more time with my family. Those kids needed me. And you know, they don't want a whole lot of time, just those important hours.

Each day, every one of us is given an allotted amount of time—24 hours, 1440 minutes, or 86,400 seconds. Whichever way we count it, we only have so much time, and when it's gone, it's gone. We will never get back one hour, one minute, or one second.

> Love *is spelled*
> *T-I-M-E*.

The life we live on this earth is all about time and what we do with it. We need to look at our time as an investment. How are you investing your time?

The Bible tells us to *"walk circumspectly, not as fools but as wise, redeeming the time, because the days are evil"* (Ephesians 5:15–16 NKJV). In essence, this passage is exhorting us to be cautious about how we live our lives and what we do with our time, not wasting it vainly on things that don't really matter.

I believe one of the best and smartest investments of our time is in our children's lives, not only for them, but for us as well. We're building a legacy that will hopefully live on long after we are gone. When we breathe our last breaths, we can't take any of our achievements and material things with us. What will really matter for us in the light of eternity are the lives we've poured ourselves into, especially our children who will grow up to affect hundreds of people. Fathers, we have a great responsibility to teach and mold our children and make the world a better place. This takes diligence, dedication, sacrifice, and *time*, but if we don't make the time we will be cheating them of the best lives they can have.

Whether they say it or not, our kids want us to post their good report cards and artwork on the refrigerator door. They want us to play one-on-one basketball games with them, practicing for the day that they finally beat us! They want us to help them rebuild that old car and teach them to fish and hunt. They want to look up and see us in the grandstands of their lives, cheering them on.

Believe it or not, they even want our rules and boundaries. But most of all our kids long for our praise and approval. And it's never too late to think of new ways to show them they're on our A-list of significant people.

Finding time is rarely easy these days. Sometimes effective fathering is like doing a circus balancing act. You ever seen one of those plate spinners? That's what it's like for us dads sometimes. Just as we get one plate spinning along steadily, we have to run and spin two others that are wobbling. By the time we get those two going strong, the first one starts to wobble. Many days, this parenting thing seems like we're running around in unending, exhausting circles. But I'm convinced the time we need is available, and the rewards will far outweigh the effort. We simply need to prioritize what's really important and make wise choices—walking cautiously, redeeming the time. Having good intentions is not enough. Those seconds, minutes, and hours are slipping away. However, if we're convicted to take time for our families and then make it a daily or weekly practice, this will eventually become a habit and a natural part of us. Good fathers realize that family time is an important and wise investment.

I can tell you that the precious moments I've invested in my children were hours, minutes, and seconds never wasted. My children have benefited, and the return of love and satisfaction that I've received has been wonderful. My wife, Joan, and I are never lonely!

At the end of your life
you will never regret
not having one more test,
not winning one more verdict,
or not closing one more deal.
You will regret time not
spent with a husband,
a child, or a parent.

BARBARA BUSH

HUG, KISS, AND TOUCH

For some fathers this may seem too difficult, but if you want to communicate love and acceptance to your kids you have to be willing to pull them close and hug them. It's also important, particularly for girls, that they understand what appropriate touch is, and Dad is the best person to model that for them. If you were never touched in an appropriate, compassionate way by your own father it might be more difficult for you to touch your own children, but if you can learn to do so, the benefits are incredible. There's nothing like a bear hug between father and son, or a loving kiss on your daughter's head, breathing in the love. Our kids need fatherly affection, no matter their ages or their gender.

Every child needs appropriate touches of affirmation. Several studies done in the 1990s and reported in *Reader's Digest* showed that the role of the father carries the most influence on the child's future for positive or negative consequences. A father's ability to deliver appropriate touches of affirmation to his children profoundly affects how children will relate to others as they grow into adulthood. Kids who've experienced positive physical affection from their father generally . . .

- feel better about themselves;
- have an easier time communicating;
- feel comfort and support;
- know they are loved.

When we talk about appropriate touching, it is important that we always respect each other's personal boundaries. Sometimes our children will not want to be touched, and we must respect those times. Appropriate touching should be:

- comfortable;
- natural;
- not showy or overdone;
- consistent;
- given freely, with nothing expected in return;
- given with their permission.

I'm Sorry, So Sorry

If we confess our sins,
he is faithful and just and will forgive us our sins
and purify us from all unrighteousness.

1 John 1:9 NIV

8

One thing I've learned in my walk with God is that confession is good for the soul. Every time I've messed up and gone to God confessing my sin to Him, He's always forgiven me. Every time, no exceptions. Like the scripture above says, "He is faithful and just and will forgive us." However, even though I know God will forgive me, sometimes it's hard for me to admit wrongdoing, and then it's even harder to go to God and tell Him I'm sorry. And the longer I cling to my sin, the more it festers inside me until I just can't take it anymore. King David knew this feeling well when he wrote, *"When I kept silent, my bones wasted away through my groaning all day long . . . Then I acknowledged my sin to you and did not cover up my iniquity. . . and you forgave the guilt of my sin"* (Psalm 32:3, 5).

Good fathers know how to admit to their kids when they've blown it, and they ask for forgiveness. "Honey, Daddy was wrong." "Johnny, I made a big mistake. Please forgive me." Telling your child, "I'm sorry. I was wrong," is not an easy thing to do. But it's amazing how powerful those few words can be in the lives of our children. I can't tell you how many mistakes I've made and how many times I've had to ask for my children's forgiveness. I've even sung songs to them like the old one by Brenda Lee: "I'm sorry, so sorry, that I acted like a fool." Once I sang that on my daughter's voicemail because she didn't want to talk to me. But something I'm discovering along this journey called fatherhood is that kids can be amazingly resilient and eager to forgive!

> *Good fathers know how to admit to their kids when they've blown it, and they ask for forgiveness.*

Choosing to *not* admit our mistakes to our kids, living like we've never hurt them, or pretending everything is fine when it's not are mistakes that injure our relationships with our children, eventually festering into sore spots that are very tender. Many adult children live in dysfunction because their parents never could admit they were wrong and ask for forgiveness. And many adult children live in bitterness because they refuse to forgive their parents. One of the most important aspects of effective fathering is the act of forgiveness—both *asking* for it and *giving* it.

Forgiveness heals relationships. Good fathers confess their wrongdoing and ask for forgiveness, and they also forgive their kids of their mistakes. They parent with a spirit of grace and humility, not judgment.

Let's talk a bit about what it means to father out of that spirit of grace and humility. Its one thing for us to admit our mistakes and ask for forgiveness, but it's quite another to expect our children to admit to us when they've been wrong. I know, it sounds like a contradiction, but we can hope that by our modeling the ability to admit wrongs and seek forgiveness, they will learn to do the same. And they will. It's just that it may take a while—possibly years.

We, as fathers, must consistently work with a spirit of patience, grace, and forgiveness even when our kids don't deserve it—like the prodigal's father did with his son and like God has done with us. Sometimes for the sake of the relationship we'll even have to let our children believe they're right without challenging them. As fathers working out of love, the relationships and issues are bigger than we are. Everything is about our kids. We have experience that gives us strength they won't have until later in their lives. We can find security in who we are as men and who we are in the Lord.

Because we often know more about our kids than they do about themselves and because we have more life experiences, we can sometimes use our accumulated wisdom as power to strip our kids naked emotionally—to really humiliate them. Don't exploit opportunities to remind them of past mistakes. Don't lord your power over them, trying to bring them down when all they're trying to do is save a little face. Romans 15:1 says, *"We who are strong ought to bear with the failings of the weak and not to please ourselves"* (NIV). This scripture not only applies to the Body of Christ, but to our children as well. Sometimes we must forgive them when they don't even realize they need forgiveness or they're not strong enough yet to admit that they need forgiveness.

> *One of the most important aspects of effective fathering is the act of forgiveness— both asking for it and giving it.*

I love to raise and ride horses. The three hundred-acre Foreman Ranch is located in the Piney Woods outside of Marshall, Texas, and is really my getaway place where I do most of my riding. Believe it or not, raising horses has taught me a thing or two about parenting and forgiveness.

Sometimes when I'm trying to help my horses, they'll kick me or step on my toes. They don't realize I'm the one who feeds and takes care of them. I'm the person who calls the veterinarian. One time a stallion bit me, causing a serious injury. I could have sold it after that. But I understood the horse didn't know what it was doing. It took its frustration out on me, because I was there.

Even though my horses are totally dependent on me, they're ignorant about how they're hurting me. So, when they try to kick me, I just overlook their outbursts and keep feeding them hay. If they really understood how their actions injured me, they would never want to hurt me again.

That's how I try to deal with my kids. They might kick me or step on my toes, but I'll choose to overlook their unknowing attacks. Most of the time kids don't get that they're hurting the very ones who are providing for them.[11] This attention is centered on themselves. It's our challenge as fathers to look past the obvious and see the hearts of our children.

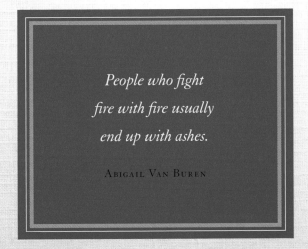

*People who fight
fire with fire usually
end up with ashes.*

ABIGAIL VAN BUREN

ROMANCE AND
HONOR YOUR WIFE

Romancing and honoring your wife is one of the most important things you can do for your children. It's something they need to see you doing! The respect they have for you will skyrocket when they watch you helping her around the house and doing things like massaging her feet. Let your wife sit on one end of the sofa and you on the other end, then have her put her feet in your lap for you to massage while you both watch TV. Your children are constantly observing how you act and how you treat others. When they see your sincere, kind demonstrations of affection toward your wife, they'll know they can expect to be treated well too. Make romancing your wife a weekly ritual, and watch your children respond . . . and watch your wife respond!

Never degrade or talk down to your wife, especially in front of your kids. Instead, build her up with praises on a consistent basis. "You know, kids, I sure married a wonderful woman! I hit a home run cause she's outta my league. And you kids are blessed to have such a mom. She's really all that!" Don't be fooled, our children hear every word and they notice how we treat one of their two most favorite people. Sometimes I'll play with my kids, just to see what they'll do, and in front of them say something to their mom like, "Hey woman, you get in here right now and fix me something to eat!" Without fail, my kids will call me down. "Daddy, don't talk to Mom like that!" I'll give them one of my big smiles and wrap my arms around their mom and just love on her. "You're right," I tell them.

It's equally important that our kids see us apologize to their mother when we've been wrong. But to do that we have to have a spirit of humility that allows us to admit our mistakes. Living with someone makes conflict inevitable sometimes. That's normal. But even during disagreements, we can choose to speak in a way that reflects our respect and love for that other person. Another point that I must add is, we must never let our children disrespect their mother either. It's important that they know we value Mom as a prize and will defend her, not tolerating anyone mistreating her, not even her children.

Don't be fooled for a microsecond. Our children are watching and they're listening. Our daughters form their image of how a man should treat them based on how their father treats his wife. Our sons learn how they should treat women by the way they see their father treating his wife. Remember, also, that to some degree our children get their image of God from their earthy father. Ephesians 5:25 encourages husbands to *"love your wives, just as Christ loved the church and gave himself for her."* That's a pretty tall order, to love our wives like Christ loved the church. How did He do that? First, He died for the church. Secondly, Christ served the church. Remember when Jesus washed the disciples' feet? That was an act of service, and we are to become loving servants to our wives. When we begin to love our wives like Christ loved, we're sure to be positive role models for our kids, and the residual benefits will be passed on from generation to generation.

THE FRIENDSHIP FACTOR

9

Two are better than one . . .
If one falls down, his friend can help him up.
But pity the man who falls and has no one to
help him up!

ECCLESIASTES 4:9–10 NIV

It's been said that a father's job is to be a parent and not a friend to their child, that kids have many friends but only two parents or, in many cases, just one. But a father must find a way to balance being both parent and friend. Our kids need to feel comfortable coming to us with their problems and whatever else is on their minds. That won't happen if we're distant and disconnected from them. We must build genuine friendships with our kids if we are going to be approachable and have a lasting impact on their lives.

When I talk about building friendships with our kids, I'm not talking about being buddy-buddy with them, trying to be like one of their peers, or making some huge effort to be the "cool" dad. Building a genuine friendship with our kids has nothing to do with any of that. It's about our children feeling empowered to be themselves around us. We want our kids to be able to shed their masks around us, letting down their guard without fear because they know that they're accepted, warts and all.

Kids are drawn to outside friendships, good ones and bad ones, for two primary reasons: (1) friends listen without being judgmental or giving too much advice and are comfortable just "hanging out," and (2) friends typically validate each other. Validation is one of the main reasons most kids are drawn to certain cliques and gangs. Often when our kids attempt to talk to us about their problems we want to "fix" them, and our approach comes across as judgmental and critical. In our honest attempts to help our kids and potentially spare them from some of the pain we've experienced, we turn them away. Remember this: to our children, unsolicited advice often comes across as criticism, and unsolicited help often comes across as control. Sometimes we need to just be able to hang out with our kids without any expectations.

A father must find a way to balance being both parent and friend.

By developing friendships with our children we eliminate fear and dread. I want my kids to feel comfortable being themselves around me and telling me their opinions, even if they think I'll probably disagree with them. Yes, I want my kids to respect and honor me, but not to the extent that it becomes fear or dread. You have to be careful with demanding your rightful respect, because you want to raise children really loving you, not fearing or resenting being around you. If your relationship slips into fear or dread, then you start driving away your kids

In addition to raising horses, I'm an amateur dog trainer. It's funny to compare what I've learned in training dogs to raising my children, but some of the comparisons are uncanny. For instance, when you are training a dog to eventually be a watchdog for your family, it's critical to start it very young and to not instill fear in the animal. It must trust you completely. If a dog becomes fearful at a young age, it's usually ruined and rehabilitation is very difficult. So, when puppies are very young, you must create a positive learning environment where they can grow. You don't want to do anything harsh that could lead to fear and anxiety in your puppies. You want young dogs to look toward a human hand as something pleasant that brings comfort, food, and affection. To create this feeling, one of the things you need to do is take time each day to gently handle each dog. Talk to it, even sing to it, while providing its care. Your consistent attention and affection will build up its confidence, and one day it will grow into a faithful watchdog. Over time, the dog has become a loyal friend. Let me tell you, a dog can innately sense when you are sincere or not. It's amazing. That type of trusting relationship is very rewarding.

Our children are much more valuable than even the most beloved family dog, and I've found with my children that it's even more important to raise them in a positive, comfortable environment that eliminates fear and anxiety. When we do, our kids become our friends and they grow up with confidence, even the confidence that lets them speak into our lives when they feel we're wrong about something. I've given my kids the freedom to say, "Hey, Dad, that's not right!"

To our children, unsolicited advice often comes across as criticism, and unsolicited help often comes across as control. Sometimes we need to just be able to hang out with our kids without any expectations.

One of the highest compliments a father can receive is for his kids to pass on to their own children the values and wisdom he has taught them. And then those children pass along the legacy to their children and so on. That's the idea. And if they love you, all the things attributed to honor and respect will happen naturally. When you really love someone, you empower them to speak into your life. The more genuine your relationship is with your kids, the safer they will feel. The safer they become, the more power they will have.

Many of the attributes of genuine friendship are really love. Here are just a few:

- Authentic friends look out for the best interest of each other.
- Authentic friends have a special tolerance for each other.
- Authentic friends set aside time to truly know each other and how each other thinks and feels.
- Authentic friends stand up for each other, for their rights and their feelings.
- Authentic friends look forward to more time together.
- Authentic friends validate and affirm.
- Authentic friends speak the truth to each other even when it hurts, are not afraid to ask each other, "What's on your mind?" and have the freedom to speak truth into each other's lives to challenge them.
- Authentic friends are on your side. They are for you.

The following story by H. L. "Bud" Tenney relates the power of a friendship between a father and son.

I had been home from work for about fifteen or twenty minutes, when my older son David came in from playing—looking very serious. He was only six years old at the time. Our younger son Mark, who is two and a half years younger, was right behind him.

I was watching the evening news on television when David

came in and stood right in front of me. I have to admit that my thoughts were rambling between the news and David. I knew he had something on his mind, and he knew he could talk to me about anything. He also thought I had the answers to everything.

As he stood there, I could sense that he was nervous and wondered if there was something wrong, or if he was just going to ask one of his very serious questions about the rules of the game they were playing. But he was much too serious for that. Now he had my full attention.

The more genuine your relationship is with your kids, the safer they will feel. The safer they become, the more power they will have.

He spoke rather quietly when he said, "Daddy, I need to talk to you."

"Okay, Davie, what's on your mind?"

"I'm a big boy now, right?"

"You sure are. Tell me what you're thinking."

He said, "I don't want you to call me 'Davie' anymore, I want you to call me 'Dave,' and I don't want to call you 'Daddy,' I want to call you 'Dad.'"

With this out, he seemed even more serious or nervous. I smiled at him with the proudest smile I think I ever had.

I said, "That will be okay, Dave. I would like to call you 'Dave' or 'David' and look forward to you calling me 'Dad.' But, don't ever call me 'Father,' okay?"

He relaxed and said in a very strong voice, "Can I go back out and play now, Dad?" As I said yes, my younger son came over close to me and said, "I still want to call you 'Daddy.'"

I said, "I'm so glad you do!"

For the next few days, every time David had anything to say to me, he would begin it with "Dad." Even if he wanted to know what we were having for supper, he would ask, "Dad, what are we having for dinner?"

It didn't take Mark long to follow suit. I could barely keep the smile off my face! My wife would turn her head to smile.

My son David died July 1, 1993. The night before he died, he and I were talking on the telephone about how he was feeling. About six weeks before, he had surgery for removal of a testicular cancer. Then they did exploratory surgery to verify that his lymph system was clear of cancer. It was, thank God.

In this telephone conversation, David told me that he was experiencing blurred vision and numbness in his fingers, as well as slurred speech. I told him that he would be alright. He had just gone back to work too soon after the surgery. He agreed and said he would slow down a bit. We both laughed, because we both knew he wouldn't slow down.

I said, "I love you, Davie,'" to which he responded with loving laughter, "I love you, too, Daddy."

I laughed and said, "Goodnight, Davie."

*"Goodnight, Daddy," he said, and we both hung up our telephones.
These were the last words we ever spoke to each other.*

*The next day at about noon, I was notified that David had been
taken by ambulance to the local hospital. His wife was with him
during the trip. When I arrived at the hospital, he was in a coma. As the
afternoon wore on, the doctor informed us that David had a ruptured
aneurysm in his brain. He lived until 7:06 P.M.*

*As I prayed for his life, many things went through my mind. Mainly,
I will forever be grateful to God for his last words. We had no fences to
mend. We enjoyed a good relationship. Although David's passing was
obviously painful—for him physically and for me emotionally—the
innocence and sweetness of that shared childhood memory offered a
poignant note on which a father can remember a son taken too early.*[12]

There is no friendship,
no love like that
of the parent for the child.

Henry Ward Beecher

GIVE YOUR KIDS
HONOR AND DIGNITY

As with the way we treat our wives, the key words here are *honor* and *dignity*. Usually we drill our children about honoring and respecting their parents. That's important. I'm definitely not trying to downplay it, but as our kids' key role models the best way we can teach them to treat others with honor and dignity is by treating them with honor and dignity.

Webster defines *honor* as an evidence or symbol of distinction. By honoring our children, we acknowledge their uniqueness, the qualities that make them exceptional. Simply put, honor is seeing our children as God sees them—precious, valuable individuals with special gifts—and then treating them accordingly.

Dignity is treating our kids with respect and common courtesy. For example, when a father needs to correct his child, he gives that child some dignity by showing self-control and not railing on him in front of his friends but instead waiting until the appropriate time. This not only gives the child dignity, but it gives the father time to think about the proper form of discipline. A good father never shames his children, stripping them of their self-respect. What we truly honor we usually also give dignity.

Some simple ways to give your children honor and dignity include:

- Modify discipline for negative behavior to each child's individual temperament.
- Set aside some one-on-one time with each child on a regular basis just to listen and get to know their world.

- Learn to value what's important to each child.
- Involve your children in important events and issues, asking them relevant questions and getting their input.
- Apologize and ask for forgiveness when you've blown it.
- Find out the best way to communicate with each child, because they are all different and have unique ways of communicating.

RELEASE YOUR KIDS TO THE LORD

*Pour out your heart like water before
the face of the Lord.
Lift your hands toward Him for the life
of your young children.*

LAMENTATIONS 2:19

10

I've always felt like my main job as a father has been to guide my kids down the right paths, to keep them in my love, and to keep them safe. One of my favorite scriptures is Matthew 23:37. It says, *"Oh Jerusalem, Jerusalem . . . how often I have longed to gather your children together as a hen gathers her chicks under her wings."* That's what I've longed to do with my children: gather them under my wings and keep them there where it's safe and secure for as long as possible. The good Lord has given me the gift to do that for them for a time, but in reality I know that regardless of how hard I try, I can't keep them there. As my children start out on their own or choose different perspectives about things, they are going to come out from under my wings, whether I like it or not.

My mama got to the point where she finally had to turn me over to the Lord and push me out of the nest, so to speak. Well, I've come full circle because I'm seeing that one of a father's main struggles is learning to *release* his children to the Lord. There's a big difference between *turning over* a child to the Lord and *releasing* a child to the Lord. *Turning over* says, "I'm exasperated by this child and have done all I can do. There's nothing left but for me to turn him over to the Lord to deal with him." Like my mama said, "George, I can't handle you anymore, so I'm turning you over to the Lord." And like I said in the first chapter, that's not a place you want to be as a young man or woman, because God's methods at that point can be harsh in order to get our attention.

Releasing our children, on the other hand, is a continual process. It's a lifestyle that begins the moment they are born and continues until the day we die. When we release our children to the Lord we understand that they are not ours even though they may bear our name and share our genetic makeup.

Our role as fathers is not that of an owner, but a privileged steward. God has entrusted us to raise them, nurture them, share our love with them, but they are not ours—in the end they go back to Him.

These beings who have so endeared themselves to our hearts are really God's property, created with specific, individual souls and minds. Our role as fathers is not that of an owner, but a privileged steward. God has entrusted us to raise them, nurture them, share our love with them, but they are *not* ours—in the end they go back to Him. Understanding this is important because it helps bring our lives and parenting into proper perspective.

I'm convinced that no one hurts like a parent hurts for their child. Neither can anyone experience the depth of love like a parent does for their child. No one except God, that is. The truth is, God loves our children more than we do; therefore, He hurts more when our children hurt. He is *the* perfect Father.

Learning to release our children to God also releases us from the pressure of trying to control every outcome regarding our kids. It also brings us more peace. Whatever season of life they're in, releasing our kids to God is a sign of our faith and trust in Him. Unless we're convinced the good Lord is in absolute control of everything, we'll be controlled by anxiety and fear.

As our children grow and as we grow as fathers, our roles are constantly changing, requiring more flexibility. Each situation we find ourselves in with our kids will require the wisdom to know when and how much to let go, when to give in and when to stand firm. Now, we get wisdom from knowing the good Lord, so as the leaders of our families we *must* be strong in our walk with God. That's the only way.

When we learn to release our kids to the Lord it becomes easier for us to release ourselves from the guilt and pain of making mistakes, which we inevitably will make because none of us is perfect. On the other hand, I also have known great parents who have tried hard to do everything right and still their child turns out to be a bad apple. I've seen families have one or more seemingly perfect children and then one child who just can't stop making poor life choices and is reaping those consequences. Those situations are difficult for any parent to endure, regardless of the child's age.

> *The most important thing a father can do for his kids is to consistently pray for them. As fathers we should not look at prayer as a last resort, but as a secret weapon!*

The ultimate aspect of releasing our kids to the Lord is becoming their prayer advocate. If you don't take anything else from this book, take this: the most important thing a father can do for his kids is to consistently pray for them. As fathers we should not look at prayer as a last resort, but as a secret weapon! Because let me tell you, things happen when we are committed to praying for our family. The Bible says, *"The prayer of a righteous man is powerful and effective"* (James 5:16 NIV). Do you really believe that? Do you really want it? I like what Stormie Omartian says in her book *The Power of a Praying Parent:* "When things go wrong in our children's lives, we blame ourselves. We beat ourselves up for not being perfect parents. But it's not being a perfect parent that makes the difference in a child's life, because there are no perfect parents. None of us are perfect, so how can we be perfect parents? It's being a praying parent that makes the difference."[13] The greatest task for us fathers is bringing ourselves and our families to God, and that can only happen through prayer. I also like what the apostle Paul wrote to the Colossians about a man named Epaphras. Paul said, "*He is always* wrestling in prayer for you, *that you may stand firm in all the will of God, mature and fully assured. I vouch for him that* he is working hard for you" (Colossians 4:12–13 NIV). Epaphras was working hard for people. What was his

When we pray for our families God not only changes them, He changes us.

work? It was wrestling in prayer. Fathers, this is what we need to be doing for our families: wrestling in prayer for them. Prayer is not some unproductive activity. It is powerful and it is God's work! When we pray for our families, God not only changes them, He changes us.

*We should speak to God
from our hearts
and talk to Him as a
child talks to his father.*

C.H. SPURGEON

*The more you pray,
the easier it becomes.
The easier it becomes,
the more you will pray.*

MOTHER TERESA

Prayer is like a
savings account at the bank.
As you keep making deposits,
the return keeps getting
bigger and bigger,
and it will be there for you
years from now.
I can assure you that
as you pray for your family,
you will reap great rewards
as the years go by.

MIKE MACINTOSH[14]

SET CLEAR BOUNDARIES

I cannot begin to fully express to fathers how important it really is to set family boundaries. In boxing, as in any sport, you can't compete unless you know the rules. Rules and regulations are in place for so many different reasons—keeping score, eliminating cheating, creating an equal playing field, promoting an atmosphere where athletes can utilize their talents—but above all, rules and regulations are in place for safety. When you take boxing out of the ring, eliminate the gloves, referees, and rules, then it becomes nothing more than street fighting where people often get killed.

Healthy boundaries are necessary for successful living and effective parenting. They provide the guidelines by which your family operates, and without them there is confusion and often harm. Boundaries promote a sense of security and strengthen the bonds of the family unit. It's difficult for anyone, especially our children, to reach their full potential without clearly defined boundaries. Rules are boundaries. When our children don't know the rules of the game they can't play successfully. If a father loves his family, he will not fear rejection when he sets boundaries.

Look at it another way. If we are purchasing a piece of property, usually the first thing we want to know is the boundary lines—if I buy this piece of land, what is legally mine? Once those lines are clearly defined, then we will know what we can do and how far we can go. If the boundary lines are not clearly defined, then that can cause all kinds of problems down the road when we are building. Likewise, unless the boundaries are set and clearly defined for our kids, they'll often be confused, not knowing what is and what's not acceptable. They'll be frustrated if one day something is okay and another day it's not. In order for us to set effective boundaries we must personally understand and follow boundaries. If you don't know what boundaries are or where to set them, you can't give guidance to your kids.

Like boxing rules, clearly defined boundaries protect our children and create an arena where they can excel. Kids thrive within clearly defined boundaries. Not setting guidelines does them a great injustice. On the other hand, defining proper boundaries helps kids, regardless of their ages, develop self-control, respect authority, function well as part of society, and feel safe and loved. Good boundaries should be:

- *Reasonable, age appropriate.* They need to be well considered and agreed upon by both parents.
- *Clearly defined.* They should be specific and clearly communicated.
- *Consistent.* All kids will invariably test our boundaries, pushing their limits. So, in addition to being clear, they must be consistently reinforced.
- *Consequence appropriate.* The severity of the discipline should be consistent with the boundary that is set.
- *Win-win.* Boundaries should benefit everyone involved. Effective boundaries create ways for both you and your kids to get what you want.
- *Positive.* The most effective boundaries spotlight the positive results of their implementation. For example: "If you are home before 11 P.M. on Friday, you can use the car on Saturday to go to the mall."

I'VE GOT MINE!
AND I'M GONE!

*Inasmuch as you did it to the least of these,
you did it to Me.*

MATTHEW 25:40 NKJV

11

After Mama turned me over to the good Lord and I had my wakeup call with the cops and their dogs, the Lord answered Mama's prayers again. That answer came in the form of an organization called the Job Corps. I basically was going nowhere fast—drinking, hanging out, getting into fights, scrambling around for odd jobs here and there—when I learned about President Lyndon Johnson's skill-learning program called the Job Corps. I had seen famous athletes, as well as All-Pro Cleveland Browns running back Jim Brown, on public-service ads inviting people like me to join. The television ads announced, "If you have dropped out of school and want a second chance at life, then the Job Corps is for you." Because Jim Brown had been one of my childhood heroes and I knew I desperately needed some direction, what he said grabbed my attention and I signed up.[15]

Once I went into the Job Corps, I came in contact with some real men with integrity who showed a genuine interest in me—retired guys from the armed forces and the coaching and teaching professions. They had within them the ingredients of authority, life experience, and love that they wanted to invest into my life. They were men who I could look up to, men I was motivated to please and emulate. I told you earlier about Charles "Doc" Broadus who was a counselor and boxing trainer. He became like a father to me. I don't know where I would have ended up if not for men like Doc. Thank God for a few men who were willing to give of themselves and take a little precious time to invest in others.

Fatherless homes are at epidemic proportions. As a result there's a whole generation of kids who lack direction.

Today, for a variety of reasons, fatherless homes are at epidemic proportions. As a result there's a whole generation of kids who lack direction, who are like I was, feeling like they're just floating around in space with nothing grounding them. There's great need for men to be surrogate fathers, men who will stand in the gap and offer positive influence, who will take some of these fatherless kids under their wings and help give them a little direction.

So, you've been raising your kids and have become pretty good at this fathering thing. That's great! I commend you, but don't put it to sleep. Obviously, never stop being a father to your own kids, but, in addition, reach out and help someone who's not biologically yours but who urgently needs your influence. America needs Big Brothers, tutors, scout leaders, coaches, and other types of mentors. If men will simply get involved, a whole nation can change. It's amazing the impact that just one man can have. Listen to Glenn Jeffery's story and let it challenge you. Glenn is the founder of an organization called Life Coaches for Kids.

Never stop being a father to your own kids, but, in addition, reach out and help someone who's not biologically yours but who urgently needs your influence.

"I became a mentor to Warren, a young man who never knew his father and whose two brothers were in a federal penitentiary. We met regularly for three years. Sometimes he was on the run, but mostly he was incarcerated in state correction facilities. Warren was considered incorrigible by the local corrections authorities. He had been running with gangs from the age of eight, stole cars, abused alcohol and drugs, and looked for love in many of the wrong places. Warren was like a lot of the kids we mentor today—totally lost, depressed, angry, trying to kill his pain with drugs, and living without much hope for the future. He had very little interest in faith. Today

Warren is the owner of a successful business, married, a good father and a leader in his church and community. When describing the reasons for his change he says, 'Someone didn't give up on me.' Warren became the inspiration for Life Coaches. Not giving up is a big part of Live Coaches for Kids. We call it caring for someone until they care for themselves, believing in someone until they believe in themselves." [16]

It doesn't take having a million dollars to be a good father to your children or to help someone who's fatherless; it just takes a willing heart and a little precious time.

Wow! We need about several million more men like Glenn Jeffery. He's a true champion in my book.

Because of my boxing career and the amazing success of the George Foreman Grill, I've been very blessed by the good Lord to make a lot of money. After I made this money, all sorts of people wanted a piece of me, and they'd tell me things like, "George, just be rich and relax. Just spend time riding your horses and traveling. Get a yacht or a jet. Just do it all!" I thought about it, and I do love my horses, but God wouldn't let me "just be rich and relax." I mean, who's going to lead? Who's going to be an example? Who's going to be a father to the fatherless? So, God led me to build the George Foreman Youth and Community Center and then take on lectures and tours promoting the need for fathers. I realized I had stumbled upon something incredibly important that could affect a whole nation and I have to share it until I die. I'm not going to buy myself out of my responsibility to help other fatherless kids. The Bible says, *"To whom much is given, much is required,"* so I just can't say, "I've got mine! And I'm gone!" Instead, I'm sticking around to help other kids get theirs.

It doesn't take having a million dollars to be a good father to your children or to help someone who's fatherless; it just takes a willing heart and a little precious time. Do you want it? Do you really want it?

A good father knows how to absorb the punches from his kids and go the distance with them.

I was coaching little league, and there was this 9-year-old named Josh, the son of a single mom. He was a big kid but he couldn't hit the ball, and he was ashamed. So I started working with him one-on-one. The next to last game of the year, Josh comes up to bat. The week before he had popped up to the pitcher with the bases loaded. He felt terrible. Anyway, he gets up, and he just creams the ball. I mean, he creams it. He starts running toward first and down toward second. I'm on third, coaching the base, and when he sees me waving him home, he looks at me—I'll never forget it as long as I live—and there are tears in his eyes. He ran home, jumped in the air, and landed with both feet on the plate. The whole dugout cleared out to hug him. Nothing replaces that. Nothing in the world. I mean, to literally change a kid. That was the best time of my life.

—JAMES CAAN, an actor who stepped away from a lucrative
film career for six years to coach his sons.[17]

Blessed indeed
is the man who hears
many gentle voices
call him father!

Lydia M. Child

ABSORB THE
FATHERHOOD EXPERIENCE

If you're going to be a boxer then you're going to get hit. That's just a fact of the sport. However, good boxers— championship boxers—can take a punch. Through proper technique, they've learned how to absorb as much of the punch as possible, eliminating most of its power. One of the reasons I won the Olympic Gold Medal and became a two-time Heavyweight Champion of the world was because I could take a punch. Being big didn't hurt, but that wasn't enough. I had to be properly trained in the art of getting hit.

Let's face it, as a dad you're going to take some punches. To be effective, you've got to learn to absorb those punches, to absorb the painful experiences of fatherhood. This means taking the pain when your child hits you with disrespectful statements that they don't mean like, "I hate you." "You don't really love me." "You're so clueless." Or when they try to manipulate and lie to you. We have to remember that our children, just like us, have a sin nature. Romans 3:23 says, *"All have sinned and fall short of the glory of God."* The word "all" in this passage includes our children. A good father knows how to absorb the punches from his kids and go the distance with them.

Fatherhood is not an easy assignment, but it has great rewards— when a daughter at nineteen still crawls up in her daddy's lap; when a son wants to be like his daddy; when a child gets that scholarship or makes the honor roll; when a child asks for your advice or simply says, "I love you Daddy." All those are great rewards, but not only do the rewards of fatherhood come through our relationships with our kids, God also uses the experience of fatherhood to teach us and develop His character in us. Simply put, God uses the parenting process as a tool to grow us into deeper, more effective men for Him. Kids have a way of humbling us. They reveal our weaknesses and show us our need for God's grace. How many fathers have, in their frustration, flung themselves on the mercy of God and cried out to Him for help? This may be hard for us, as men, to accept, but it's right where God would have us to be, desperately dependent upon Him. Absorbing the fatherhood experience is about letting God use daily situations with our kids as tools to shape us.

A Note about My Father and God's Amazing Grace

12

And the grace of our Lord was exceedingly abundant, with faith and love which are in Christ Jesus.

1 TIMOTHY 1:14

I want to encourage you that if your father is still living, never give up on your relationship with him, regardless of how rocky or distant your past may have been. God's grace truly is amazing, and God specializes in restoration of broken relationships. As I've told you in this book, my father, J. D. Foreman, was an alcoholic and left our family when I was very young. I would see him from time to time stumbling in the streets and quite often would be embarrassed. Our family did everything to try to get him to quit drinking, but nothing worked.

One day after I was a grown man and had become a minister for the Lord, I was street preaching and realized that my father had been standing at a distance listening. Not long after that, he showed up at my church. Well, the short version is that J. D. Foreman got radically saved and totally set free from alcohol. He continued to attend my church for the remaining years of his life. We became great friends, and I got my father back! Remember, with God, it's never too late.

I hope this little book has been an encouragement to your soul. Thanks for reading it!

ENDNOTES

[1] Steve Farrar, *Anchor Man* (Nashville: Thomas Nelson, 1998), 29.

[2] Ken Canfield, *The Heart of a Father* (Chicago: Northfield Publishing, 1996), 17.

[3] Kathy Peel, *Family for Life* (New York: McGraw Hill, 2003), 100–102.

[4] Farrar, *Anchor Man*, 97.

[5] Brennan Manning, *The Ragamuffin Gospel* (Sisters, Oregon: Multnomah, 2000), 182.

[6] George Foreman, *God in My Corner* (Nashville: Thomas Nelson, 2007), 11.

[7] Foreman, *Corner*, 118.

[8] Foreman, *Corner*, 118.

[9] Marjorie Holmes, *How Can I Find You, God?* (New York: Doubleday, 1975), 6.

[10] Mother Teresa, *The Joy in Loving* (New York: Viking, 1997), 82.

[11] Foreman, *Corner*, 73.

[12] "Last Words" from *Chicken Soup for the Father's Soul*, edited by Jack Canfield, Mark Victor Hansen, Jeff Aubery, Mark Donnelly, and Chrissy Donnelly. Copyright © 2001 by H. L. "Bud" Tenney. Reprinted with the permission of Health Communications, Inc., www.hcibooks.com.

[13] Stormie Omartian, *The Power of a Praying Parent* (Eugene: Harvest House, 1995), 28.

[14]Mike Macintosh, *Falling in Love with Prayer* (Colorado
  Springs: Cook, 2004), 146.

[15]Foreman, *Corner*, 10.

[16]Glenn W. Jeffrey, *Life Coaches for Kids* online newsletter, April
  2007, p. 3. www.lifecoaches.org.

[17]Joe Kita, *The Father's Guide to the Meaning of Life* (Rodale
  Books, 2000), 115.

ABOUT THE AUTHOR

GEORGE FOREMAN, twice boxing's heavyweight champion of the world, is best known today as an entrepreneur and philanthropist. He is a frequent speaker at events nationwide. George is an ordained minister who preaches twice a week in his church in Houston, and he is the father of ten children.

If you enjoyed *Fatherhood by George*, try these other powerful books.

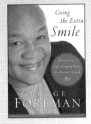

Going the Extra Smile: Discover the
Life-Changing Power of a Positive Outlook
   When it comes to a positive, can-do attitude, George Foreman is the champ, and he shares personal stories and key insights about achieving victory in the ring of life. $12.99 hardcover, ISBN 978-1-4041-0419-8.

God in My Corner: A Spiritual Memoir
George Foreman is one of the most highly recognizable figures on the planet, and he reveals how God has been behind the scenes of every part of his life. $22.99 hardcover, ISBN 978-0-8499-0314-4; $14.99 trade paper, ISBN 978-0-8499-1989-3.

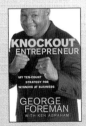

Knockout Entrepreneur: My Ten-Count Strategy
for Winning at Business
What George Foreman has learned from his best and worst times as a boxer and a businessman can help make you a knockout entrepreneur too. $22.99 hardcover, ISBN 978-0-7852-2208-8.

The righteous man
walks in his integrity;
His children
are blessed after him.

PROVERBS 20:7

NOTES